D0124288

W9-BTC-232

A Picture Book of
Simón Bolívar

David A. Adler
illustrated by Robert Casilla

Holiday House / New York

To Elliot and Jessica
D.A.A.

To my son, Robert Jr.
R.C.

Library of Congress Cataloging-in-Publication Data
Adler, David A.
A picture book of Simón Bolívar / by David A. Adler :
illustrated by Robert Casilla.
p.   cm.
Summary: A brief biography of South America's great soldier and
patriot who led many countries out from under Spanish dominance.
ISBN 0-8234-0927-9
1. Bolivar, Simón, 1783–1830—Juvenile literature.
2. Heads of state—South America—Biography—Juvenile literature.
[1. Bolívar, Simón, 1783–1830.   2. Heads of state.   3. South America—History.]
I. Casilla, Robert, ill. II. Title.
F2235.3.A745   1992   91-19419   CIP
980′.02′092—dc20   AC
[B]

Other books in David A. Adler's
Picture Book Biography series

A Picture Book of George Washington
A Picture Book of Abraham Lincoln
A Picture Book of Martin Luther King, Jr.
A Picture Book of Thomas Jefferson
A Picture Book of Benjamin Franklin
A Picture Book of Helen Keller
A Picture Book of Eleanor Roosevelt
A Picture Book of Christopher Columbus
A Picture Book of John F. Kennedy
A Picture Book of Harriet Tubman

Simón Bolívar was born in Caracus, Venezuela, on July 24, 1783.

It was a time of great revolutions. In the year of his birth, the Treaty of Versailles was signed, giving the thirteen American Colonies their independence from England. Six years later, in 1789, the French Revolution began.

During Bolívar's childhood, the people of Venezuela had no voice in how their country was ruled. Venezuela was a colony of Spain. It was governed by Peninsulares, people born in Spain who lived in Venezuela. Creoles, people born in South America to families that had come from Spain, couldn't run their own country, but they owned much of the land. Indians and blacks were mostly poor and they had fewer rights than the Creoles. The many slaves in Venezuela had the least rights of anyone.

Juan and María Bolívar

Simón's parents, Juan and María, were very wealthy Creoles. They had a beautiful house in the city and another home in the country. They owned copper and silver mines, huge herds of horses and cattle, and sugar, cocoa, and indigo plantations. They also owned more than one thousand slaves.

Simón was the youngest of four children. His brother Juan and his sister Juana were quiet, with blond hair and blue eyes. Simón and his sister María were loud and sometimes difficult, with dark curly hair and black eyes.

When Simón was three, his father died. Six years later his mother died, too. He was raised by his uncle, and by Hipólita, a slave who was like a mother to him.

Juan

Juana

María

Simón

Simón was nervous, always moving. One of his private teachers called him a "keg of dynamite." When Simón heard that, he warned his teacher to keep away. "I might explode," he said.

When Simón was nine, Simón Rodríguez was hired to teach him. Rodríguez was often in trouble. He had run away from home when he was fourteen and wandered through Europe. Many people thought he was strange, but he was an excellent teacher for Simón. He taught Simón that all people are equal and should be free; that people should choose their own rulers and make their own laws.

In Venezuela and in other colonies, there were the beginnings of revolts against Spanish rule, especially among the underclasses. The rebel leaders were caught, tortured, and killed by Spanish soldiers. Their dead bodies were often put on display to warn others not to fight.

In 1797 there was a plot to throw the Spanish out of Venezuela. It was discovered, and Simón's tutor, Rodríguez, was involved. He was forced to leave the country.

Simón had lost his beloved teacher. He joined a military troop. Then, in 1799, he went to Spain to live with relatives and to study.

In Madrid, the capital of Spain, Simón met María Teresa de Toro, a gentle, charming young woman. Simón later wrote, "My head was filled with mists of love." They were married in May, 1802, and Simón's new wife returned with him to Venezuela.

Simón's great happiness did not last. Just a few months later, María Teresa became ill with yellow fever. She died in January, 1803.

Alexander von Humbolt

Simón was just nineteen years old and already his father, mother, and wife had died. He was filled with grief and unhappy at home, so he traveled to Spain, France, Italy, England, and the United States.

In Paris, France, Simón met some very important people. One man, Alexander von Humboldt, a famous German scientist and explorer, told him that Venezuela was ready for independence.

With the loss of his wife and with all that he had learned on his travels, Bolívar was a changed man. When he was in Italy with his former teacher, Rodríguez, Bolívar swore that he would free his country from Spain.

Simón returned to Venezuela in 1807. In 1808 Napoleon Bonaparte, the emperor of France, and his large army marched into Spain and took over the kingdom. There was constant fighting in Spain, and, in the Colonies, there was talk of revolution. On April 19, 1810, the Spanish governor was forced out of Venezuela. Governors of other Spanish colonies were forced out, too.

"We are determined to be free!" Simón Bolívar told the *junta*, the council of rebels ruling the country. Two days later, on July 5, 1811, the *junta* declared Venezuela independent from Spain. Now they had to fight for their independence.

The fight for independence went on for ten years in Venezuela and even longer elsewhere in South America. Simón Bolívar became a leader in the fight against Spain.

In the early years of the revolution there were some terrible defeats. In March 1812 an earthquake in Caracus killed some ten thousand rebels while the Spanish forces were mostly unharmed. Many people saw this as a sign that God was fighting on the side of the Spanish king. Bolívar didn't. "If nature is against us," he said, "we shall fight it and force it to our will."

Bolívar formed a new army, and in August 1813 he liberated Venezuela. Less than one year later the Spanish won it back.

In 1815 Bolívar resigned from his position as a military leader. He escaped from the Spanish to the safety of the British island of Jamaica, but he did not forget his homeland. In one letter he wrote, "Whatever my fate, my last breath will be for my country." In his famous "Jamaica Letter," he wrote his thoughts about the history and future of South America. He hoped to see it become the "greatest nation in the world" because of its "freedom and glory."

Bolívar continued to fight. In February 1819 Venezuela was not yet free from Spain, but Simón decided it was time to form a democratic government. He was elected its president. Bolívar had freed his family's slaves five years earlier. Now he called for all slaves in Venezuela to be set free, but they were not freed until many years later, in 1854.

In August 1819 Bolívar had one of his greatest victories. He led his troops through rivers and lakes, and over the Andes Mountains to the neighboring country of New Granada. There he surprised and defeated the Spanish in the Battle of Boyacá.

Bolívar united New Granada and Venezuela into a new country called Gran Colombia. He was elected its president.

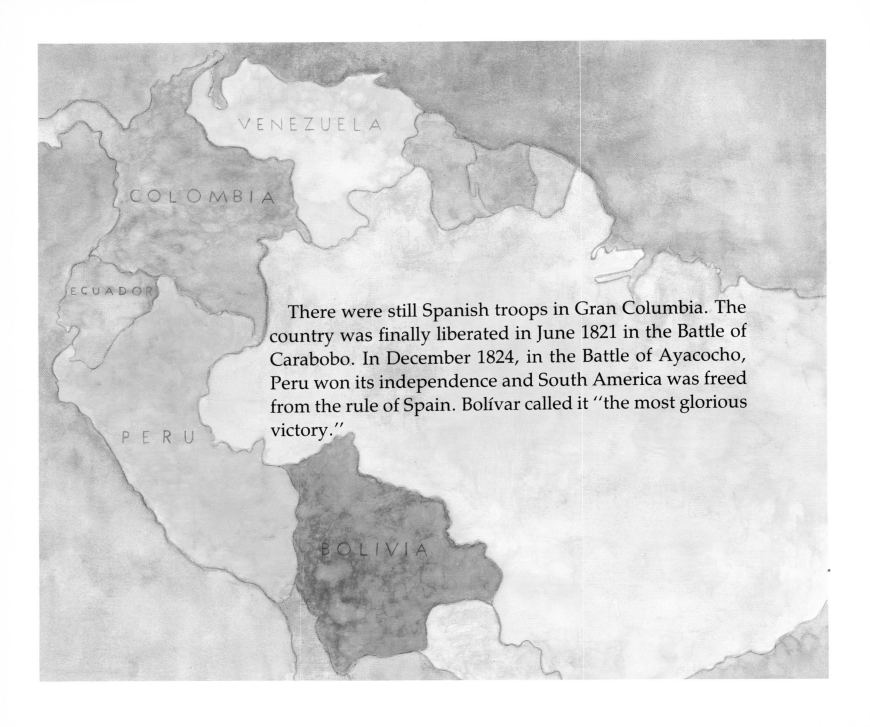

There were still Spanish troops in Gran Columbia. The country was finally liberated in June 1821 in the Battle of Carabobo. In December 1824, in the Battle of Ayacocho, Peru won its independence and South America was freed from the rule of Spain. Bolívar called it "the most glorious victory."

Bolívar was honored. He became known as *El Leberta-dor* (The Liberator) and the "Second Washington of the New World." He had hoped to form a United South America, but the lands he liberated would be many nations, not one. Today Venezuela, Colombia, Ecuador, Peru, and Bolivia honor him as their liberator. Bolivia was named for him. Dollars in his native Venezuela are called Bolívars.

The great plantations and houses Bolívar once owned had been destroyed during the fight for independence. During the last years of his life he was a poor man.

Simón Bolívar died of tuberculosis on December 17, 1830. Shortly before that he wrote, "My last wishes are for the happiness of my country."

Simón Bolívar was a great soldier and a patriot. He led his people through rivers, over mountains, and into battle. He led them to independence.

IMPORTANT DATES

1783   Born on July 24 in Caracas, Venezuela.

1786   His father died.

1792   His mother died.

1799   Traveled to Spain.

1802   Married María Teresa de Toro.

1803   His wife, María Teresa, died on January 22.

1811   Venezuela declared itself independent from Spain on July 5.

1819   Defeated Spanish forces at the Battle of Boyacá on August 7.

1821   Defeated Spanish forces at the Battle of Carabobo. Venezuela was liberated. Elected president of Gran Colombia at the Cúcuta Congress.

1824   Spanish forces defeated at the Battle of Ayacucho. Peru was liberated in this final defeat of Spain in South America.

1830   Died of tuberculosis in Santa Marta, Colombia, on December 17.